SUPER SPACE
STICKER ACTIVITY BOOK

Pull out the sticker sheets and keep
them by you as you complete each page.
There are also lots of extra stickers to
use in this book or anywhere you want!
Have fun!

NATIONAL GEOGRAPHIC
Washington, D.C.
Consultant: Peter Ricketts
Editorial, Design, and Production by
make believe ideas

Picture credits: All space artwork by David Aguilar/National Geographic unless noted as follows. Corbis Images: 11 ml; Fotolia: 10 tl; Make Believe Ideas: 11 br, 21 tl, tr, 22 br; NASA: 1 br (star cluster); NASA/ESA/STScI, 3 tl (elliptical galaxy): Optical: NASA/ESA/STScI/M. West X-ray: NASA/CXC/Penn State/G. Garmire; tr (spiral galaxy): NASA, ESA, and the Hubble Heritage (STScI/AURA)-ESA/Hubble Collaboration, 4 tr (star cluster): NASA/ESA/STScI, 5 bl (black hole): NASA/ESA and G. Bacon (STScI), 8, 9 m (sun): ESA/NASA/SOHO, 12 tl (ISS): NASA JSC2006-E-43519, 14 bl (Saturn's ring): NASA/JPL/University of Colorado; bm (rock x4): NASA/JPL, 15 bl (moon landing): NASA/AS11-40-5875; br (Buzz Aldrin): NASA, 17 ml (Venus's surface): NASA/JPL, 19 bm (Curiosity): NASA/JPL-Caltech, 20, 21 (spread background): NASA, ESA, and the Hubble Heritage (STScI/AURA)-ESA/Hubble Collaboration, 28 m; ml (asteroid x2): NASA/JPL-Caltech; m (asteroid Eros x2): NEAR Project, NLR, JHUAPL, Goddard SVS, NASA, 31 m (Voyager): NASA, 34 tm (ISS): NASA; bm (ISS): NASA/0101424, 35 br (cupola): NASA/ISS022-E-066972, 36 br (robonaut): NASA/JSC Robert Markowitz, 37 bl (Hubble space telescope): NASA; br (Earth): NASA, 38 ml (Jupiter's moons): NASA, 40 ml (Carina Nebula): NASA, ESA, and M. Livio and the Hubble 20th Anniversary Team (STScI); Shutterstock: 1 tr, 2, 3 (background), 5 tm, 6 tm, 8, 9 (background), 10 ml, 11 tm (background); m (rocket x3); bl; br, 12 ml (maze planet), 12, 13 (background), 14 ml, 15 tl (background), 17 tm (background), 21 tm, 28 tm, 29 ml, 30 tr, 32, 33 (spread background), 33 tm (space background), 35 br, 36 tm.

Sticker pages: All space artwork by David Aguilar/National Geographic unless noted as follows: ITF: 10, 11 fish: orange-and-white. yellow: Make Believe Ideas: 4, 5. socks: apple: basketball, 6, 7 eagle: bear: wolf. 10, 11 fish: yellow-black-and-white, gray; rattlesnake; leopard gecko; albatross; polar bear x2; squirrel monkey; frog; tiger; camel, 24, 25 apple; dinosaur; saxophone, 30, 31 beagle, 36, 37 present; dinosaur; pineapple; alarm clock; flashlight; saw; hammer; cheese; NASA: 4, 5 white dwarf: NASA/JPL-Caltech/Univ. of Ariz.; supernova: NASA, ESA, J. Hester, A. Loll (ASU], 14, 15 asteroid x4: NASA/JPL-Caltech; asteroid Eros x4: NEAR Project, NLR, JHUAPL, Goddard SVS, NASA; moon landing: NASA/AS11-40-5875, 16, 17 Venus: NASA/JPL, 18, 19 Phobos: NASA/JPL Caltech/Univ. of Ariz.; Deimos: NASA/JPL-Caltech/Univ. of Ariz.; Curiosity: NASA/JPL-Caltech, 22, 23 Saturn's rings: NASA/JPL/University of Colorado, 24, 25 Triton: NASA/JPL, 28, 29 asteroid x2: NASA/JPL-Caltech; asteroid Eros x2: NEAR Project, NLR, JHUAPL, Goddard SVS, NASA; Halley's comet: NASA, 34, 35 astronaut (m): NASA/GPN-2000-001156, 36, 37 Io: NASA/JPL/Uni. of Ariz., 40 Carina Nebula: NASA, ESA, and M. Livio and the Hubble 20th Anniversary Team (STScI); Shutterstock: 4, 5 robot, 6, 7 sun, 10, 11 bannerfish, 12, 13 dish antenna x3, 14, 15 astronaut, 16, 17 Mercury, 20, 21 Jupiter's moons x3, 22, 23 Titan, 26, 27 Pluto x2, 30, 31 astronaut: helmet, gloves x2, boots x2, 32, 33 space food x3; astronaut, 34, 35 astronaut x2; Earth from space.

Printed in China. 20/MBI/6

What's in our Universe?

Finish stickering this spiral galaxy!

Scientists believe the universe began 14 billion years ago with the big bang.

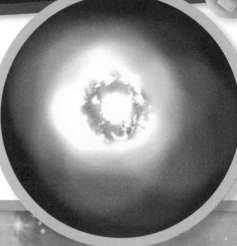

big bang

Sticker the planets in our solar system.

sun

Mercury

Venus

Earth

Mars

2

Sparkly stars and constellations

black hole

white dwarf

supernova

Stars are huge, burning balls of gas.

The hottest stars appear blue, while cooler stars are red or orange.

Color the hot and cool stars.

Draw the other half of these stars!

Stars form patterns that we call constellations.

Connect the dots to form constellations.

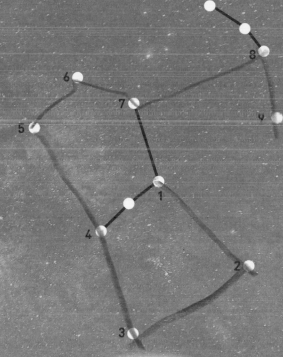

Hercules

Big Dipper

Orion

When some stars die, they become black holes!

What's been sucked into the black hole?

Sticker more stars.

5

Our sun is a star!

The sun gives us heat and light. Without the sun, there would be no life on Earth.

Sticker animals on Earth!

Find your way to the sun's core then get back home.

Start

Core

Home

6

The sun is a star that orbits the center of the Milky Way galaxy.

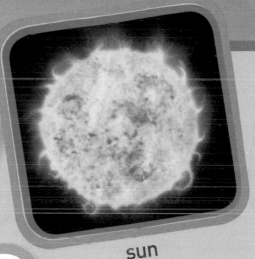

sun

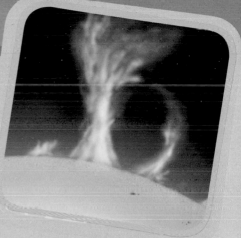

solar flare

Can you find the sun that's different?

How hot do you think the sun is? Color the thermometer.

Use your stickers to finish the picture of the sun's surface.

Super hot!

Boiling hot!

Very hot!

Hot

Warm

Cool

Cold

Freezing

Inside our solar system

Many objects orbit the sun: the eight planets, comets, an asteroid belt, and several dwarf planets.

Sticker the planets in their orbits and add more asteroids!

Uranus

Jupiter

Venus

Mercury

The asteroid belt is a ring of millions of rocky objects that lies between Mars and Jupiter.

Neptune

Mars

Saturn

sun

Earth

Earth

The planets in our solar system are known as rocky planets or gas giants!

ROCKY

Earth

Venus

Mars

Mercury

GAS GIANTS

Saturn

Jupiter

Neptune

Uranus

Earth is our home.

core

lower mantle

Below its surface, Earth is made up of different layers.

upper mantle

Color Earth's layers!

crust

Draw your family on Earth.

Sticker more fish in the ocean.

Oceans cover 70 percent of Earth's surface.

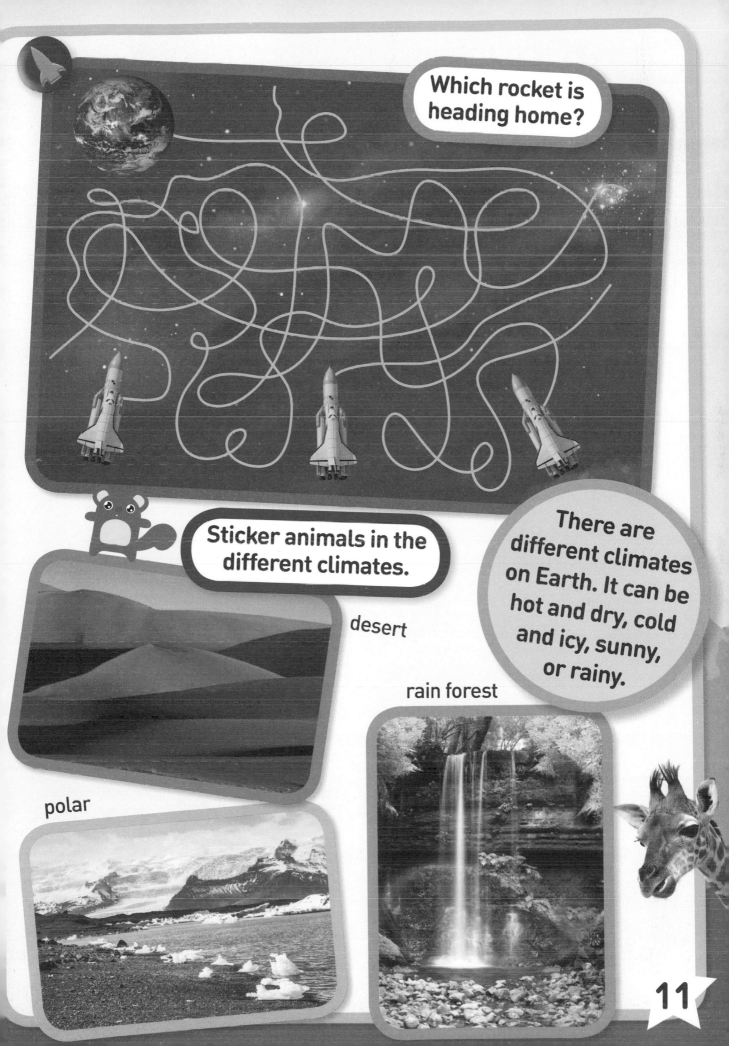

Which rocket is heading home?

Sticker animals in the different climates.

There are different climates on Earth. It can be hot and dry, cold and icy, sunny, or rainy.

desert

rain forest

polar

The sky is filled with satellites!

A satellite can be natural, like a moon, or man-made, like a space station.

International Space Station

moon

Help the spaceship travel to Earth.

Start

Earth

Sticker more dish antennas!

The **moon** orbits around Earth.

Sticker asteroids and draw more craters on the moon.

The moon's craters are made by asteroids and comets hitting the surface.

Sticker more rockets flying through space!

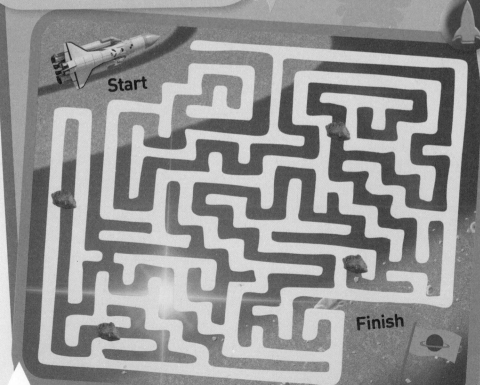

Start

Finish

Help the rocket get through the maze without hitting any asteroids.

The moon is 4.5 billion years old—about the same age as Earth.

Draw a ship landing on the moon.

Find the missing astronaut.

Twelve people have walked on the moon. Buzz Aldrin and Neil Armstrong were the first, in 1969.

Buzz Aldrin

Finish stickering the moon landing!

Explore Mercury and Venus!

Mercury

Mercury orbits very close to the sun and its surface can reach 801°F (427°C)!

Venus orbits closer to the sun than Earth does, so one year on Venus takes just 225 Earth days.

Venus

Sticker Mercury and make your way there!

Mercury

Imagine a vacation on Mercury. What would you pack?

×

One day on Mercury would last about 176 Earth days.

Who is heading to Venus?

Venus's surface

There are more than 1,600 volcanoes on the surface of Venus.

Decorate Venus with volcanoes!

17

All about Mars

Could we live on Mars one day? Design your own Martian home.

Sticker Mars's two moons.

Some scientists think there was once life on Mars.

Phobos

Sticker more Martians!

Find the alien that's different.

Connect the dots and color the Martian!

The surface of Mars is rocky and uneven.

crater on Mars

The Curiosity rover landed on Mars in 2012 and is still recording data for scientists!

Finish building the Curiosity rover to explore the surface of Mars!

19

Jupiter is the largest planet!

You could not stand on Jupiter because, unlike Earth, Jupiter is made mostly of gas!

Find your way through Jupiter's swirling gas!

Great Red Spot

Start

Finish

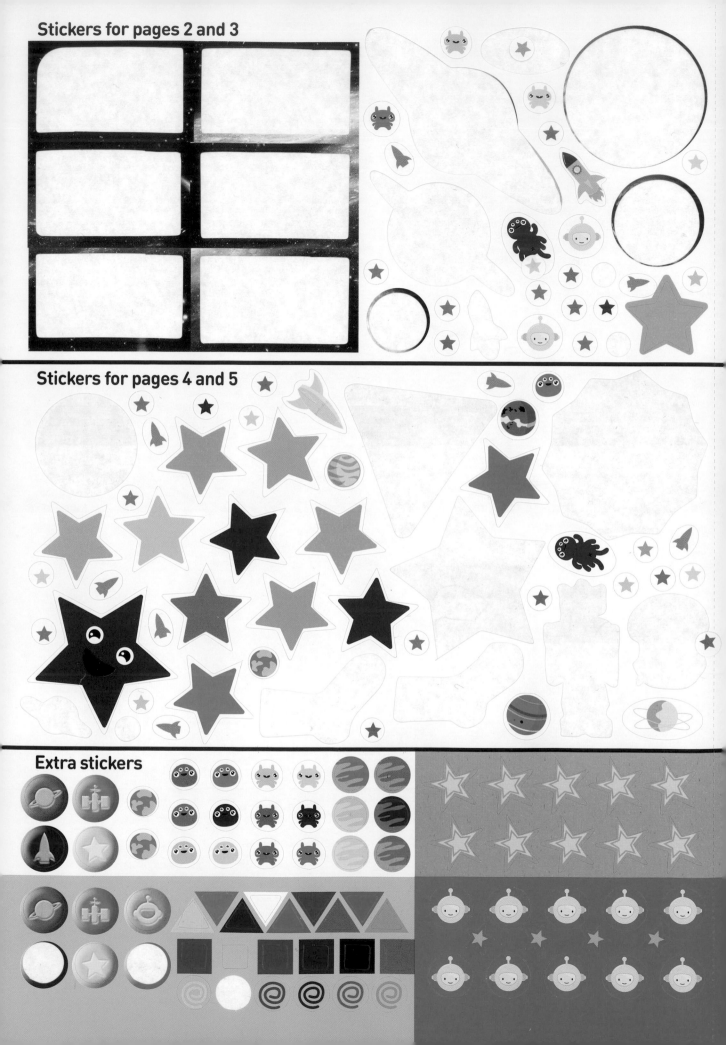

Stickers for pages 2 and 3

Stickers for pages 4 and 5

Extra stickers

Stickers for pages 6 and 7

Stickers for pages 8 and 9

Stickers for pages 10 and 11

Stickers for pages 12 and 13

Extra stickers

Stickers for pages 14 and 15

Stickers for pages 16 and 17

Stickers for pages 18 and 19

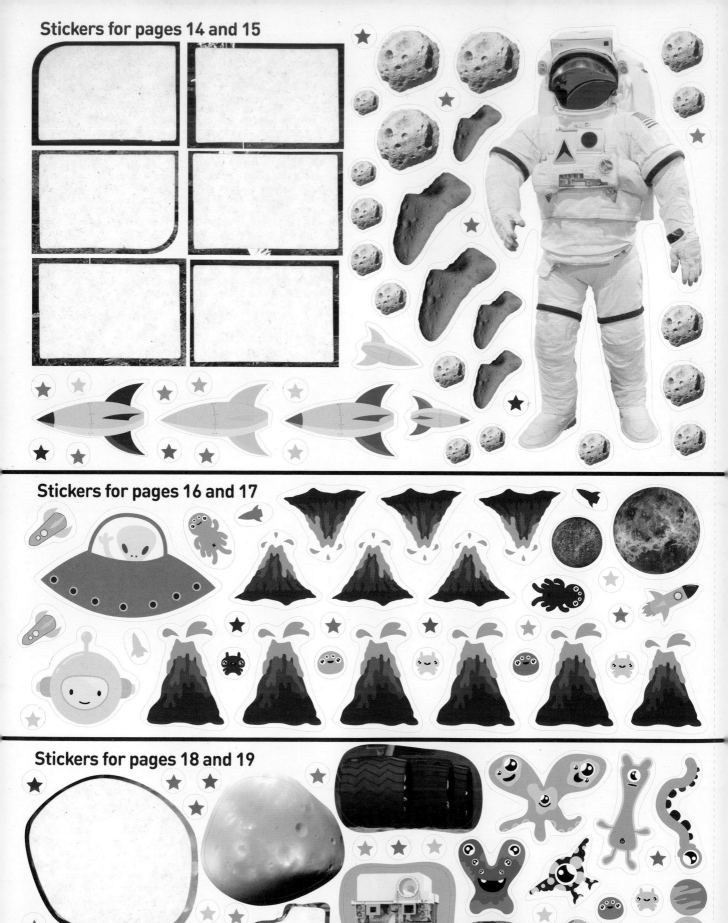

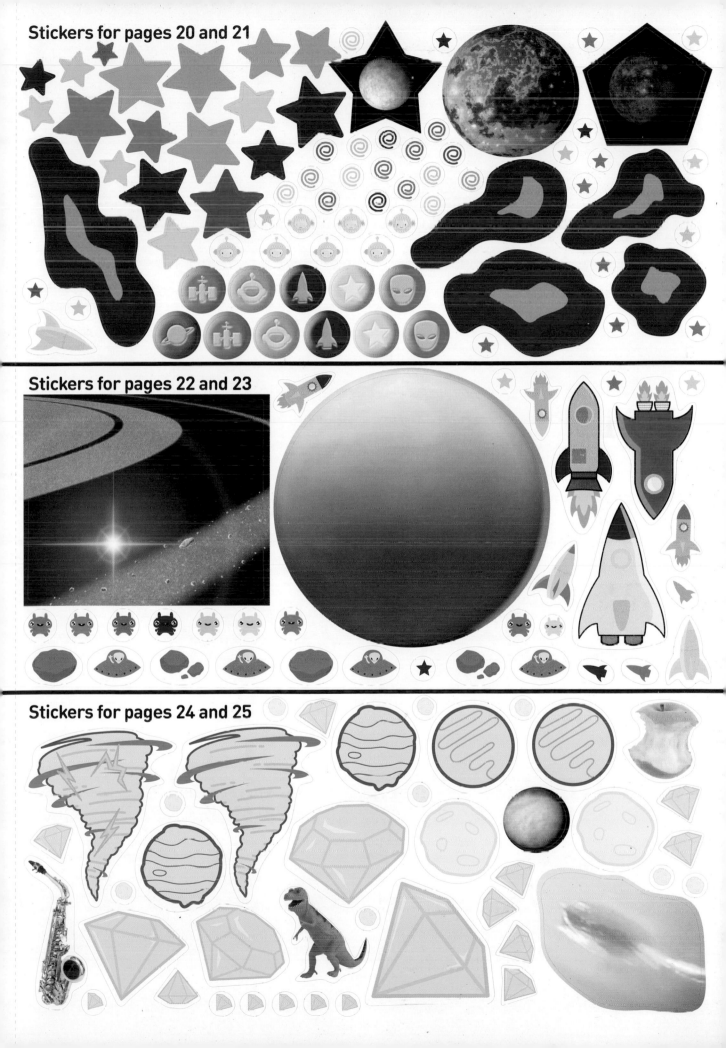

Stickers for pages 20 and 21

Stickers for pages 22 and 23

Stickers for pages 24 and 25

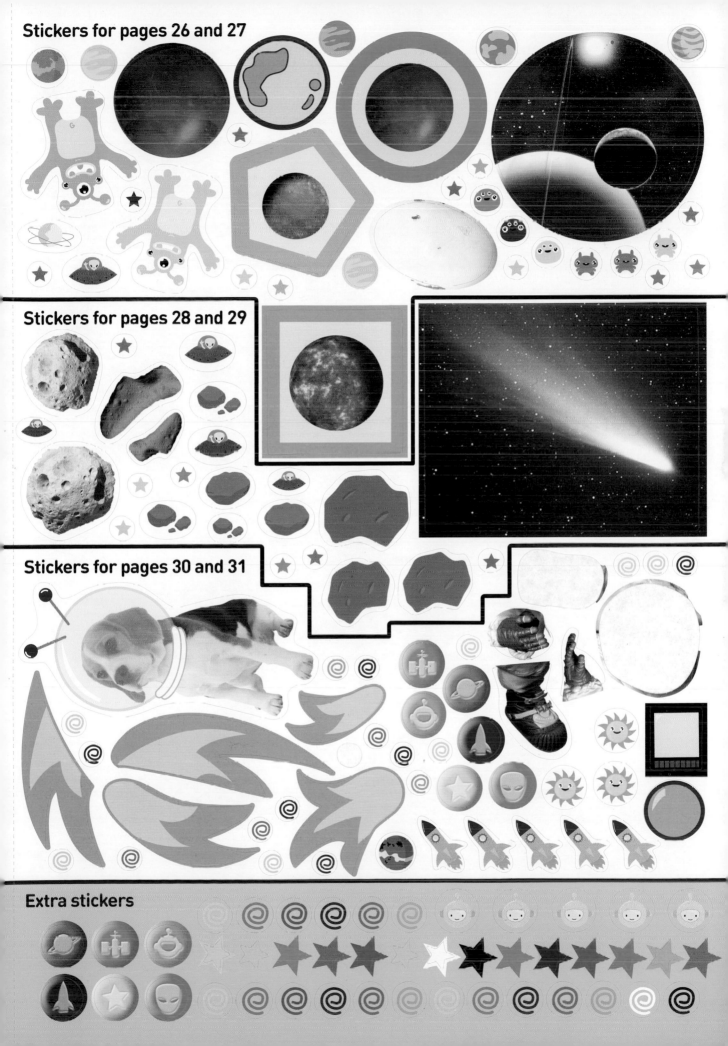

Stickers for pages 26 and 27

Stickers for pages 28 and 29

Stickers for pages 30 and 31

Extra stickers

Stickers for pages 32 and 33

Stickers for pages 34 and 35

Extra stickers

Stickers for pages 36 and 37

Stickers for pages 38 and 39

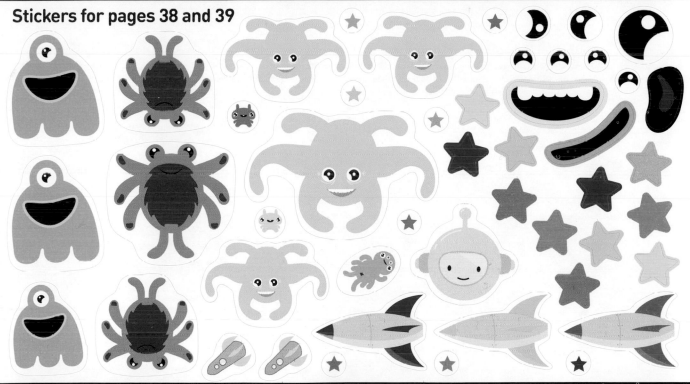

Stickers for page 40

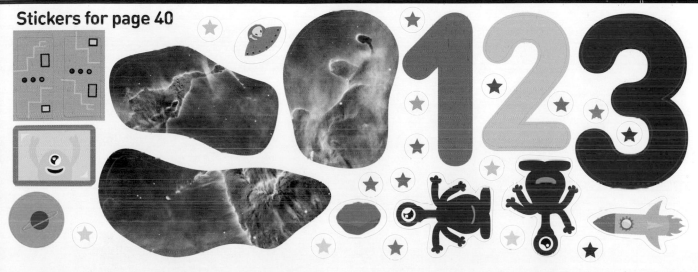

Saturn has lots of rings!

Saturn has three main rings, made of floating chunks of water, rocks, ice, and dust.

Saturn's rings

Draw what an alien from Saturn might look like!

Because it is made mostly of gas if you put Saturn in a gigantic bucket of water, it would float like an iceberg!

Decorate Saturn's rings!

Who's flying to Saturn?

Titan is the second largest moon in our solar system next to Jupiter's Ganymede.

Titan

Check out Uranus and Neptune!

Uranus is bright blue-green because of the methane gas in its atmosphere.

Uranus has 27 known moons. Finish these moon patterns.

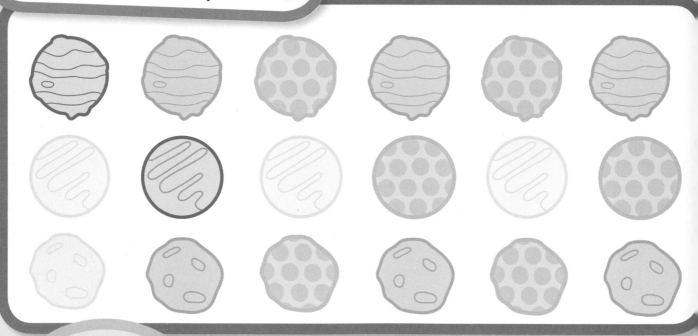

Scientists think there could be oceans of diamonds on Uranus and Neptune!

Sticker a sparkling diamond ocean.

Neptune's Great Dark Spot was a storm about the size of Earth, with the fastest winds in the solar system. It disappeared in 1994.

Sticker storms and find the one that's different.

Color Neptune.

Sticker Neptune's biggest moon, Triton.

Sticker what is lost in Neptune's storms!

Neptune has many huge storms that can last a few years at a time!

Explore other planets in space!

Dwarf planets orbit our sun, but they are not planets or moons.

Eris

Ceres

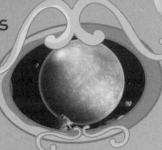

Haumea

Pluto

Makemake

Pluto

Makemake

Eris

Which dwarf planet does the alien live on?

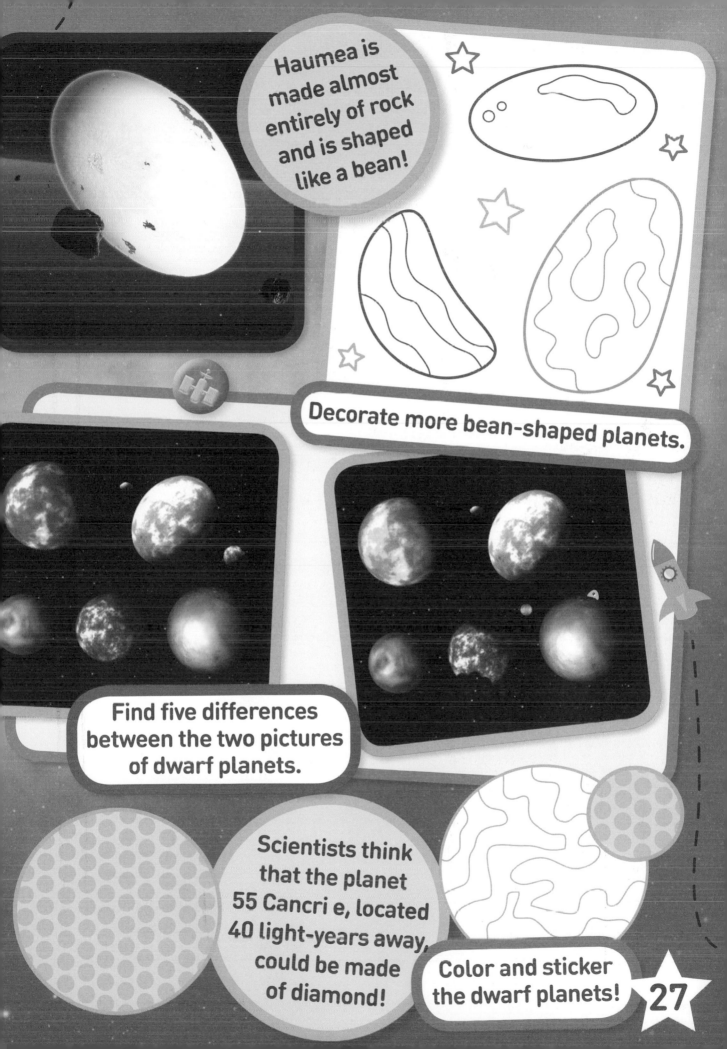

Haumea is made almost entirely of rock and is shaped like a bean!

Decorate more bean-shaped planets.

Find five differences between the two pictures of dwarf planets.

Scientists think that the planet 55 Cancri e, located 40 light-years away, could be made of diamond!

Color and sticker the dwarf planets!

Flying asteroids, meteors, and comets!

The asteroid belt is shaped like a donut ring! It contains thousands of chunks of rock called asteroids.

Asteroid belt

Sticker and draw more asteroids in the asteroid belt.

shooting star

Shooting stars look like flashes of light flying across the sky. They are made up of pieces of ice and rock called meteors.

Color the shooting star!

Comets are a mix of ice, dust, and rock.

Connect the dots and then color the telescope that's used to see the comet from far away.

Hale-Bopp

Halley's comet

Hale-Bopp and Halley's comet are called great comets. They are bright enough to be seen without a telescope.

Draw your own comet!

29

Blast off!

Color a blasting rocket!

More than 500 people have flown into outer space. Yuri Gagarin was the first, in 1961.

Find the missing stickers to finish the astronaut.

Color the rocket controls and sticker the missing buttons!

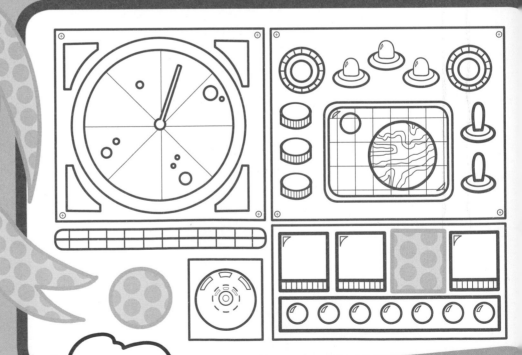

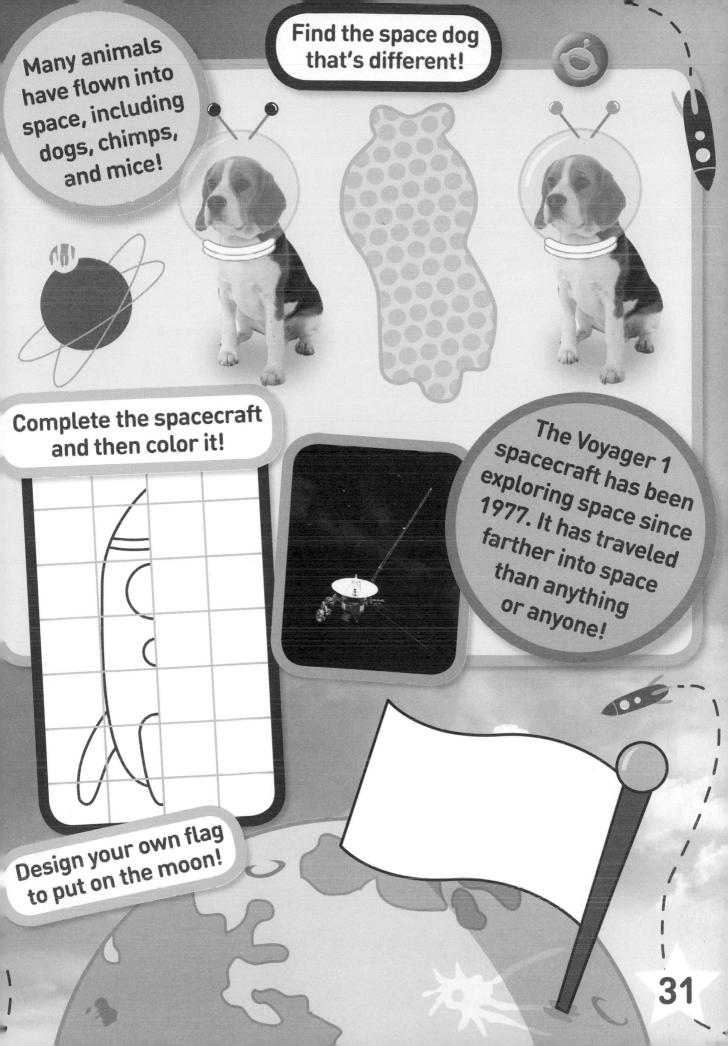

Many animals have flown into space, including dogs, chimps, and mice!

Find the space dog that's different!

Complete the spacecraft and then color it!

The Voyager 1 spacecraft has been exploring space since 1977. It has traveled farther into space than anything or anyone!

Design your own flag to put on the moon!

31

Living in space!

Decorate this supersuit!

Sticker and draw food for the astronaut.

Astronauts don't eat crumbly food like bread because the lack of gravity in space means the crumbs would float around!

Which astronaut is going on a space walk?

Help the astronaut get through the spacecraft to find the ice cream.

A space walk is when an astronaut leaves the spacecraft to make repairs or do other work in space.

Start

The International Space Station

The ISS flies more than 200 miles (320 km) above us and can be seen from Earth at night.

Sticker astronauts living and working on the ISS.

Sticker what else is flying around the ISS!

34

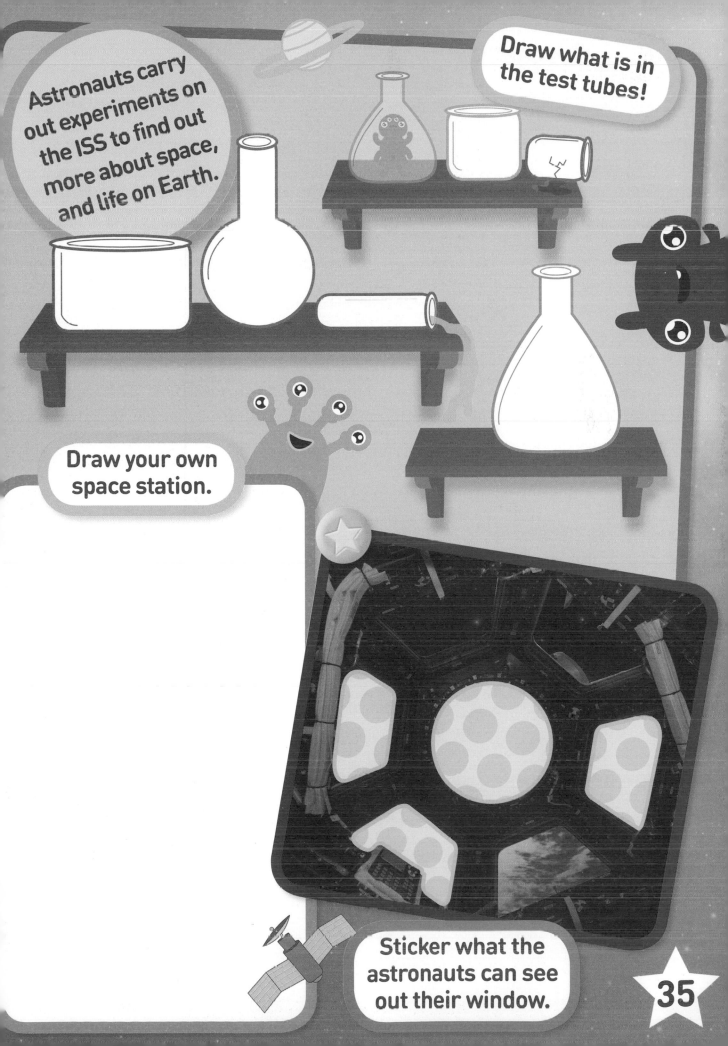

Astronauts carry out experiments on the ISS to find out more about space, and life on Earth.

Draw what is in the test tubes!

Draw your own space station.

Sticker what the astronauts can see out their window.

35

Super space gadgets!

Robots can be sent into space to take pictures, search for water, and take rock samples.

Sticker what the robot has found!

Robonauts can use tools to do jobs that are too dangerous, or even too boring, for astronauts!

Sticker and color to finish the robonaut's toolbox.

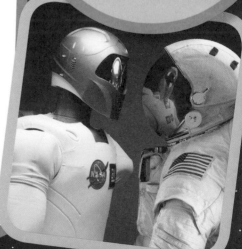

Start

Earth

Help the spacecraft get back to Earth.

Sticker what the Hubble telescope can see.

37

Are we alone?

Scientists think that alien life might exist in the ice-covered oceans on Jupiter's moon Europa.

Jupiter's moons

Connect the dots to discover an icy alien!

Start

Finish

Help the alien get to its ship!

Sticker and draw funny faces on the aliens!

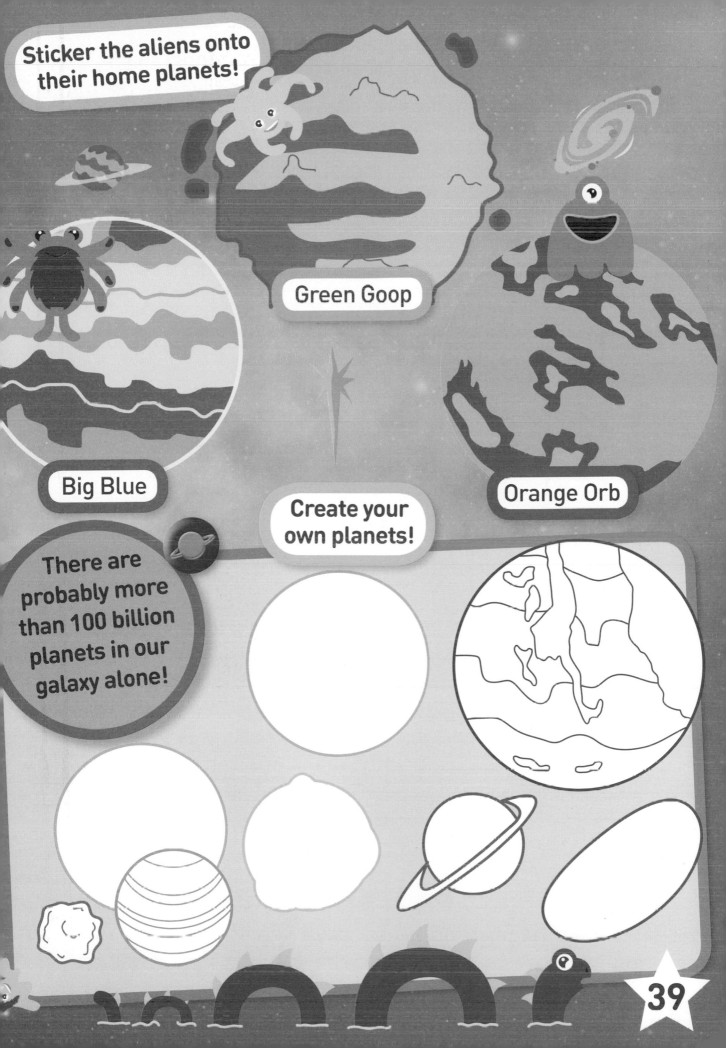

Sticker the aliens onto their home planets!

Green Goop

Big Blue

Orange Orb

Create your own planets!

There are probably more than 100 billion planets in our galaxy alone!

39

Imagine **yourself** in **space!**

Color your spaceship.

Sticker and color your rocket.

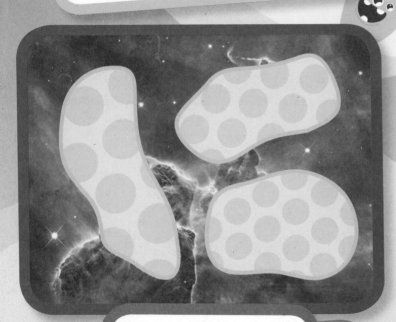

Finish the nebula.

Find the rest of the alien family!

BLAST OFF!

40